D1682964

ACTIVITY GATO ©

All rights reserved. This book or any portion thereof may not be reproduced or used in any manner whatsoever without the express written permission of the publisher.

You can contact us

activitygato@gmail.com

You can find our other books (more than 50 other books) on Amazon by typing «activity gato book»

© 2021 ACTIVITY GATO

If you don't want to become a dinosaur dish, you have to adapt to this dangerous environment.

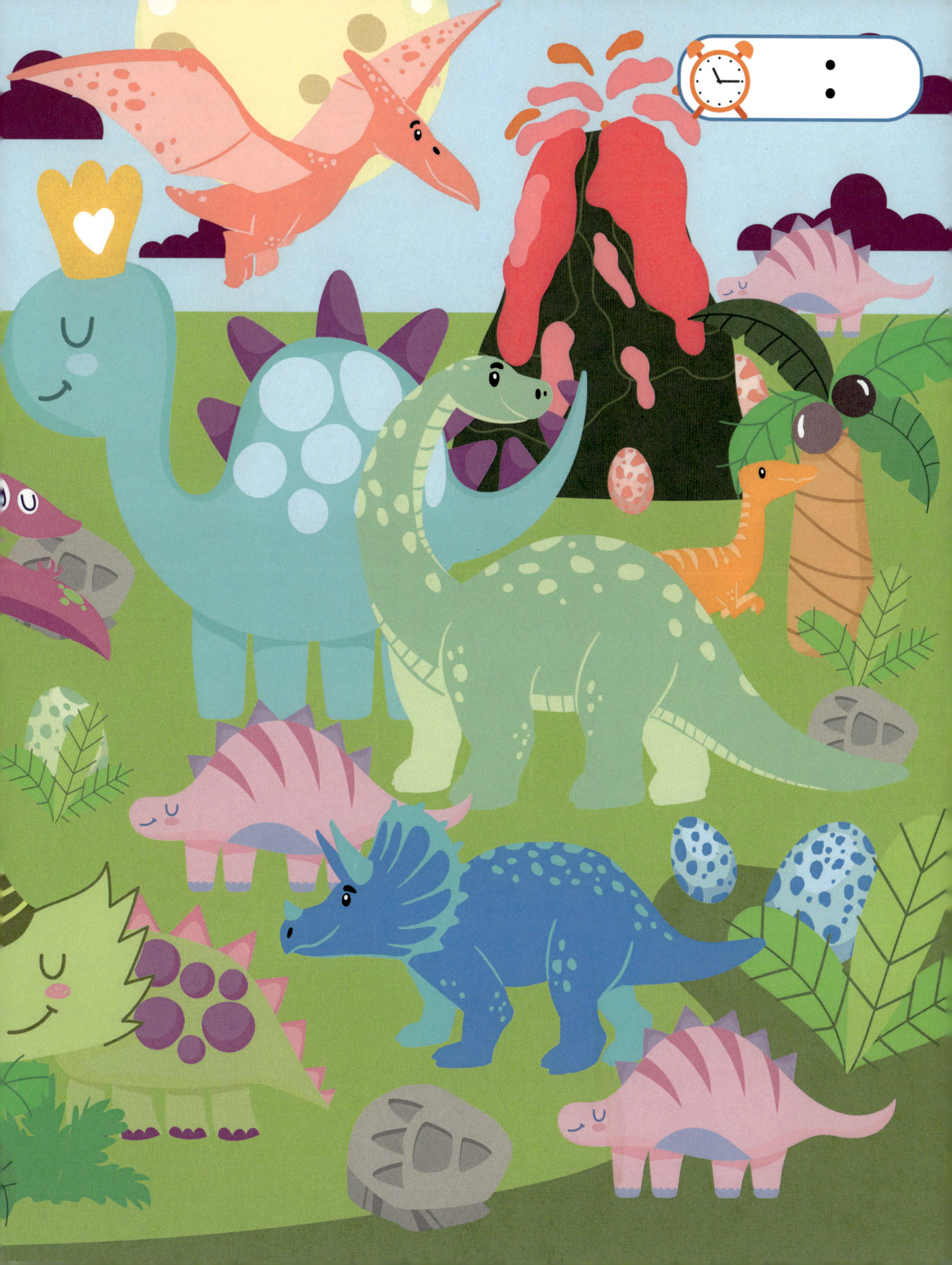

You can measure how long it takes you to find everything and mark it in the upper right corner. You can then challenge your classmates.

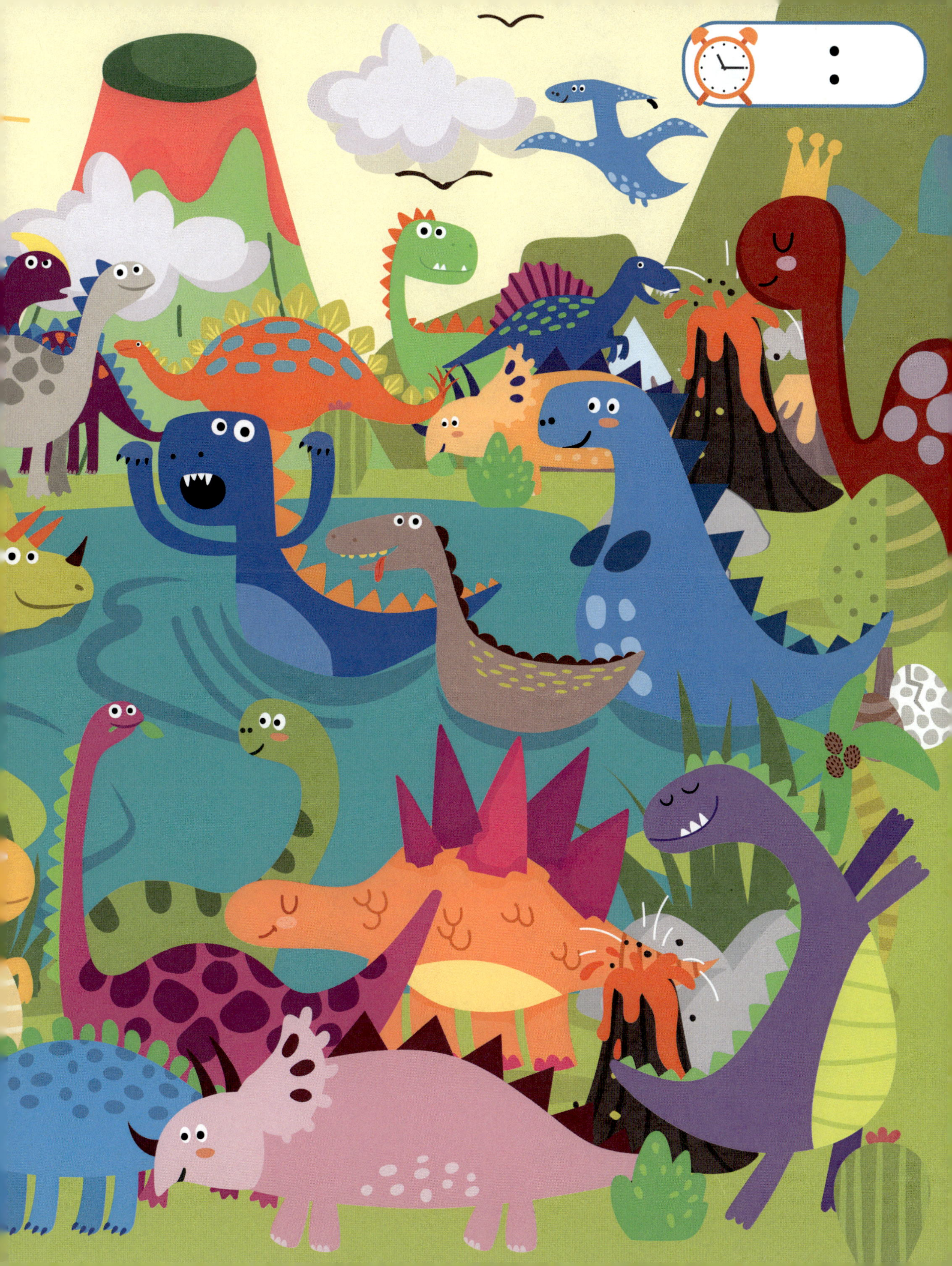

4
4
3
3
3
3
5

In reality, humans and dinosaurs never lived together, we did not ride them, nor keep them as pets or harness them for domestic labor.

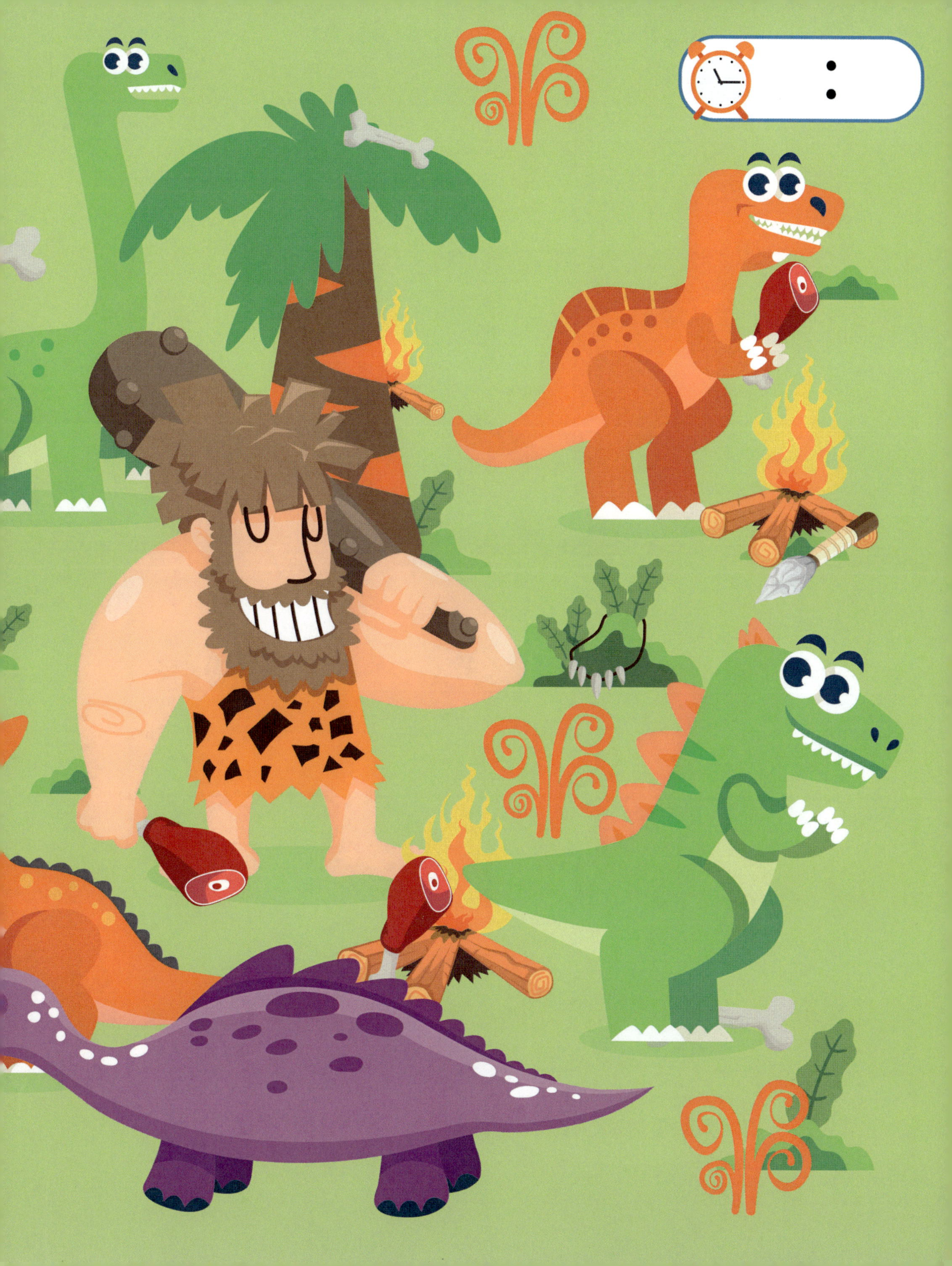

How many types of dinosaurs were there?

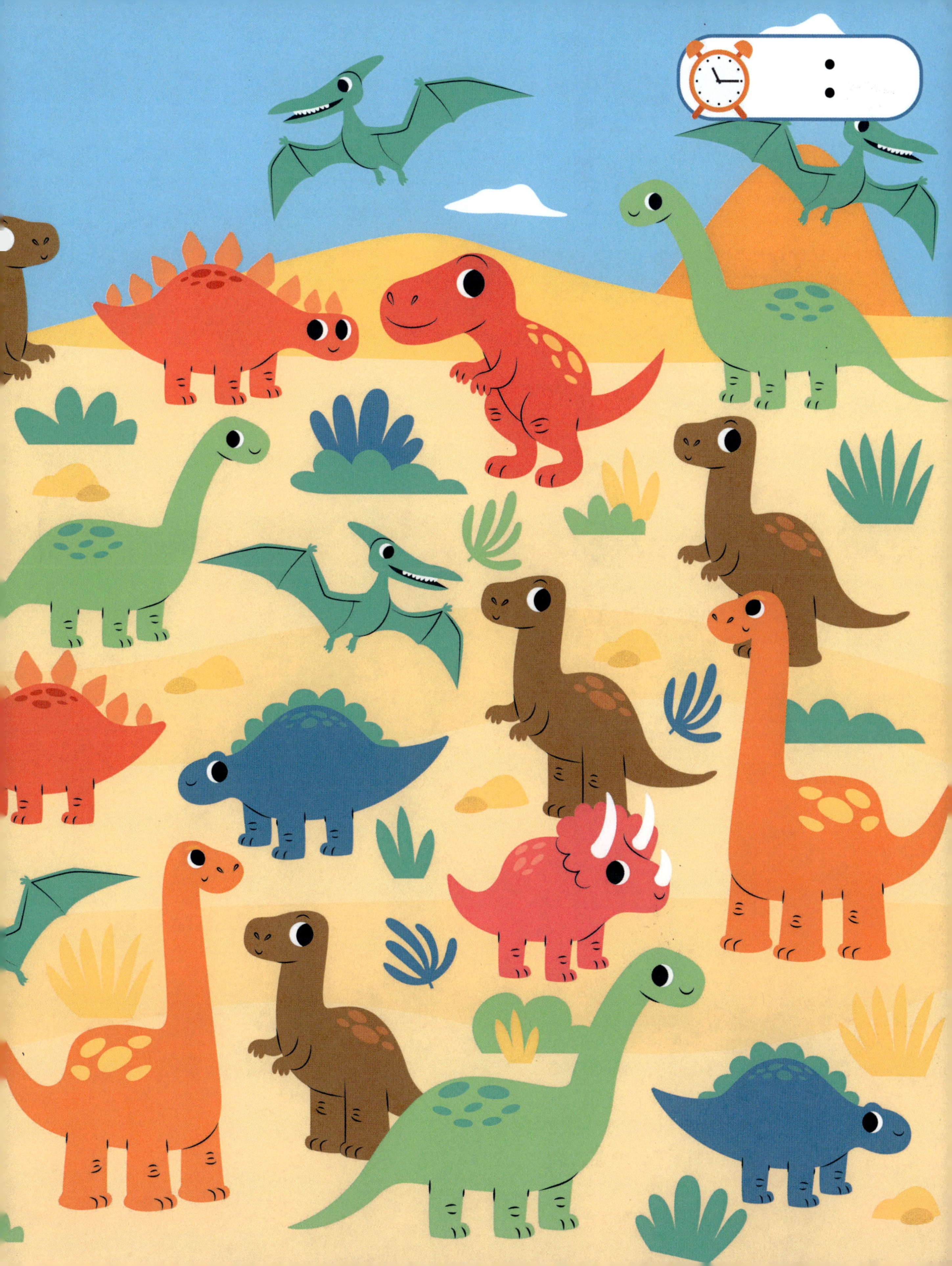

Today, birds are classified in the group of dinosaurs. So they are related to these dinosaurs!

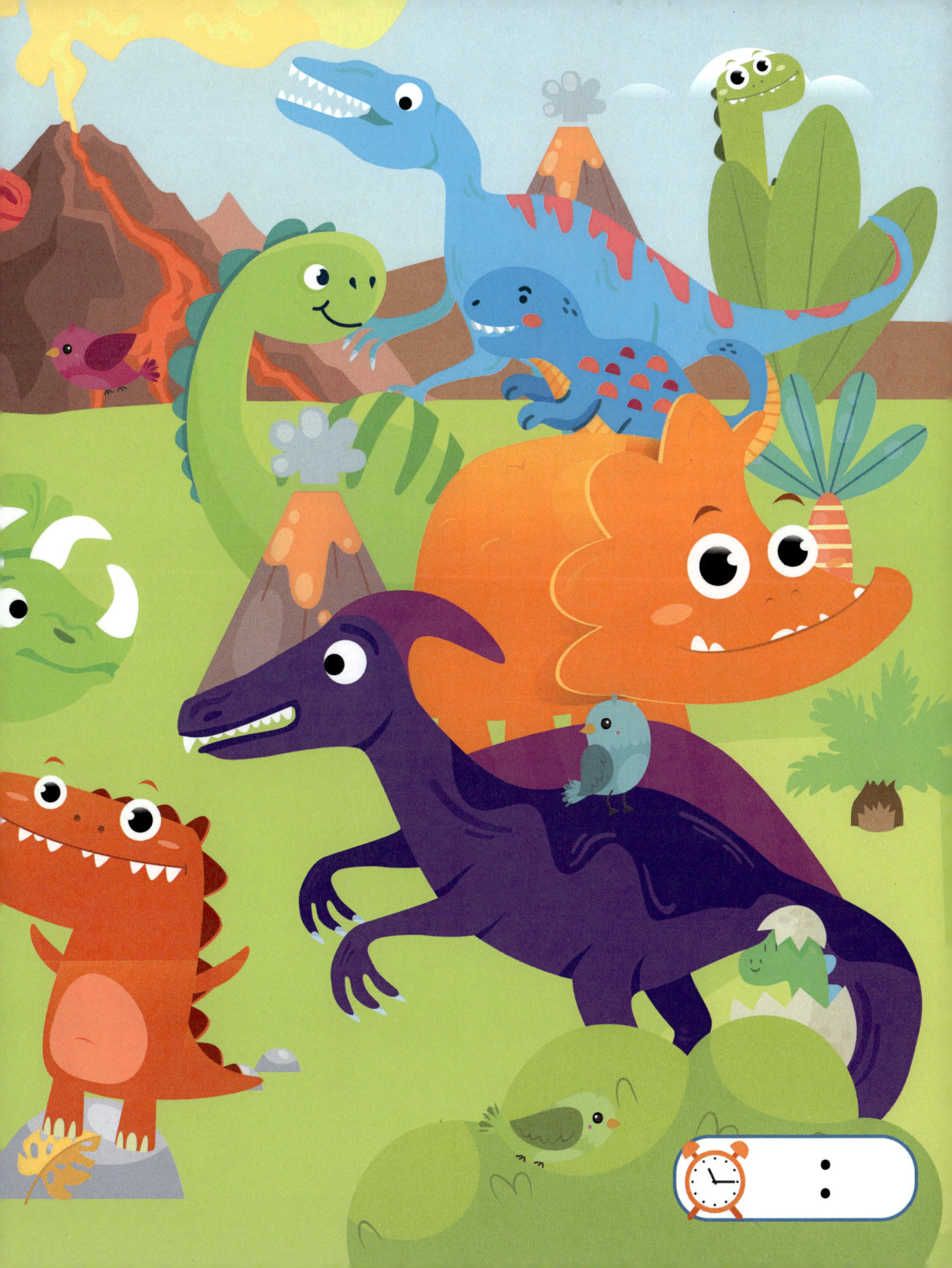

It is by studying fossils that we know what the dinosaurs looked like.

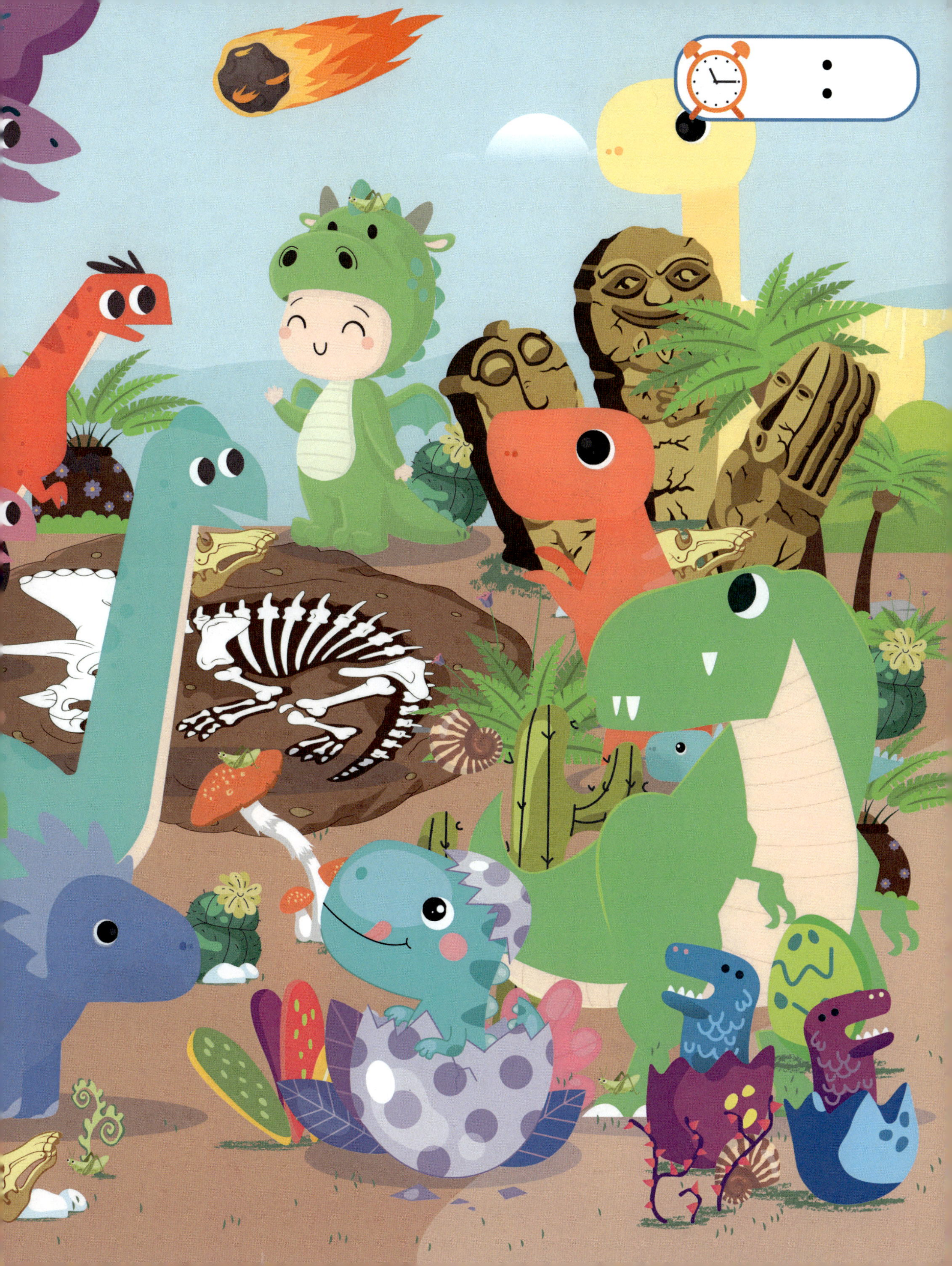

4

7

The dinosaurs are oviparous, which means they laid eggs to have their young ones.

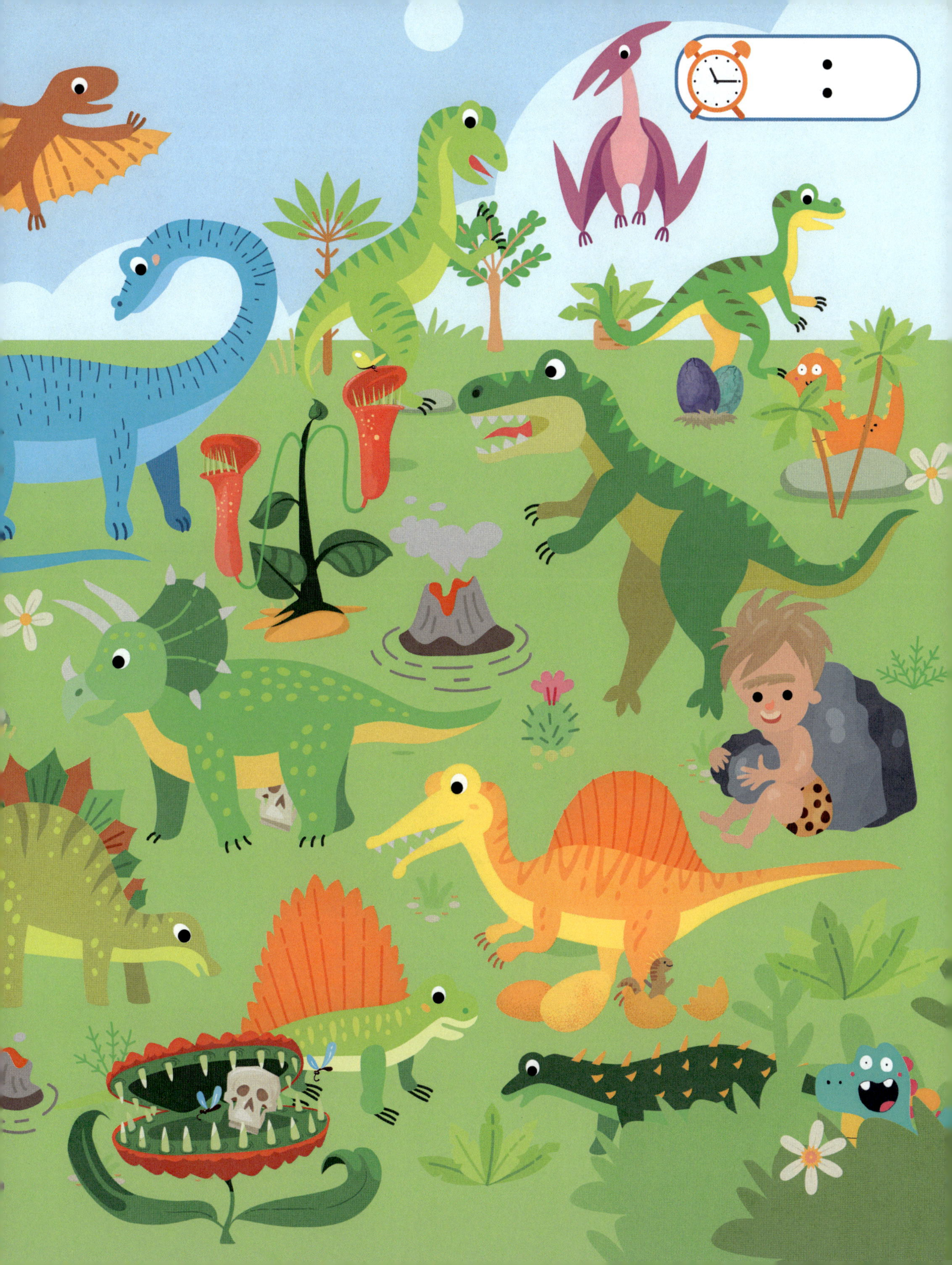

TYRANNOSAURUS REX (T-REX)

By far the best-known species of dinosaur. He was the largest carnivore in its area. His arms are so small that they can't even touch!

VELOCIRAPTOR

It is a nimble, carnivorous dinosaur with long claws.
It is known for its high speed, given that it can go as fast as a car in town. (40 km/h) or 25 mph.

PTERODAKTYLUS

It is a flying reptile, not a dinosaur, although it lived at the same era.

TRICERATOPS

It is a herbivorous dinosaur with a huge and hard skull adorned with three horns. Triceratops lived in herds.

It's time to learn how to recognize the most famous dinosaurs that roamed the Earth.

DIPLODOCUS

This herbivorous dinosaur is giant. Its neck and tail are very long.

ANKYLOSAURUS

It's a herbivorous dinosaur covered with a defensive armor of bone plates and thorns all over its back. It had a strong clubbed tail which was useful in its defence.

PARASAUROLOPHUS

The Parasaurolphus had an unusual tail that was tall but narrow. It is thought these could have been brightly colored and used to communicate.

STEGOSAURUS

It's a herbivorous dinosaur. The main distinguishing mark of the Stegosaurus is its back with two vertical rows of bony plates that impress enemies.

2 TRICERATOPS

1 ANKYLOSAURUS

1 STEGOSAURUS

2 PTERODAKTYLUS

4

Your turn !

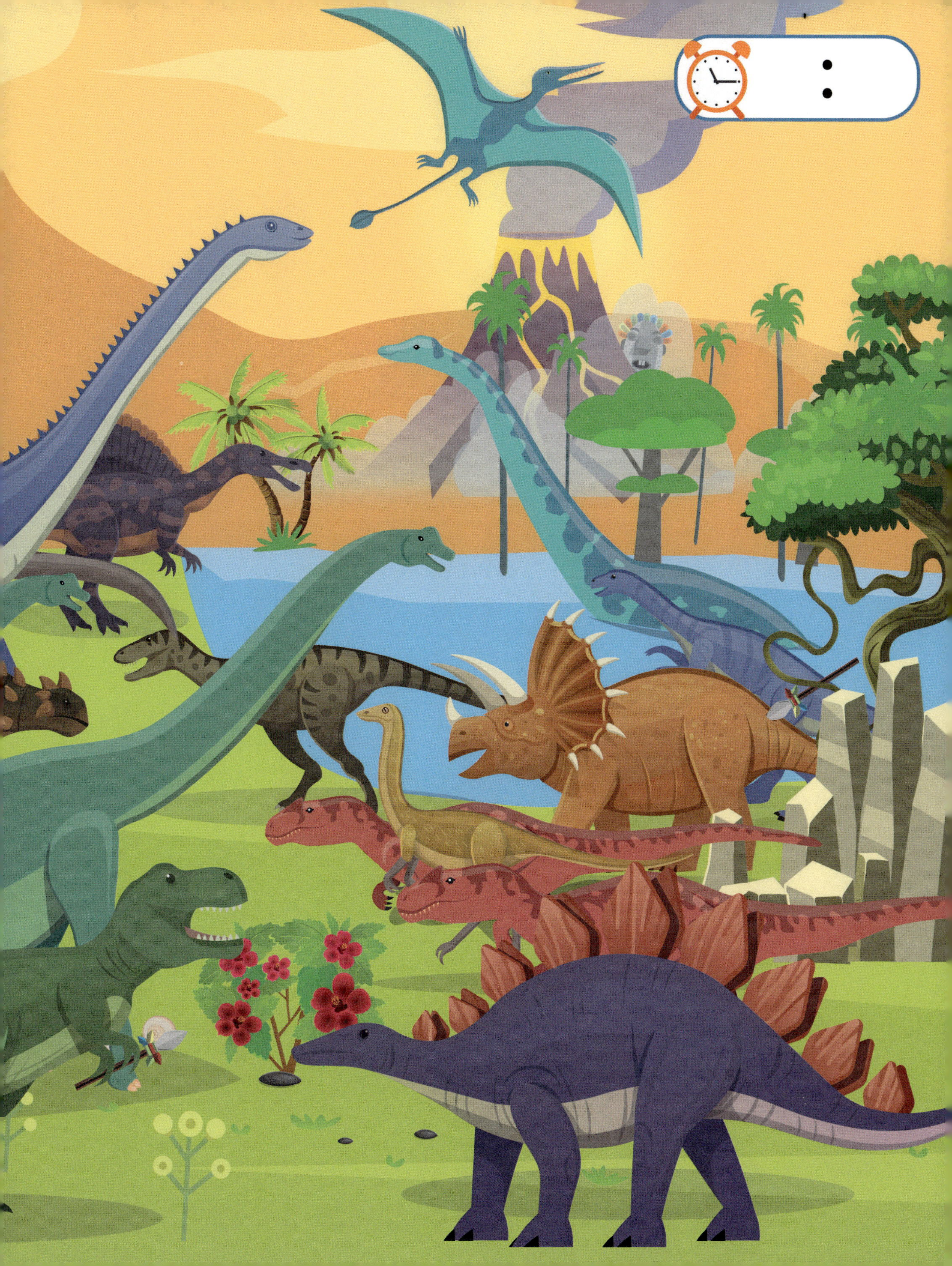

2 STEGOSAURUS

3 🕷

3 🦋(moth)

2 🐛

4 🦋

In the past, insects were much larger than today. Some even exceeded one meter in length (40 inch)

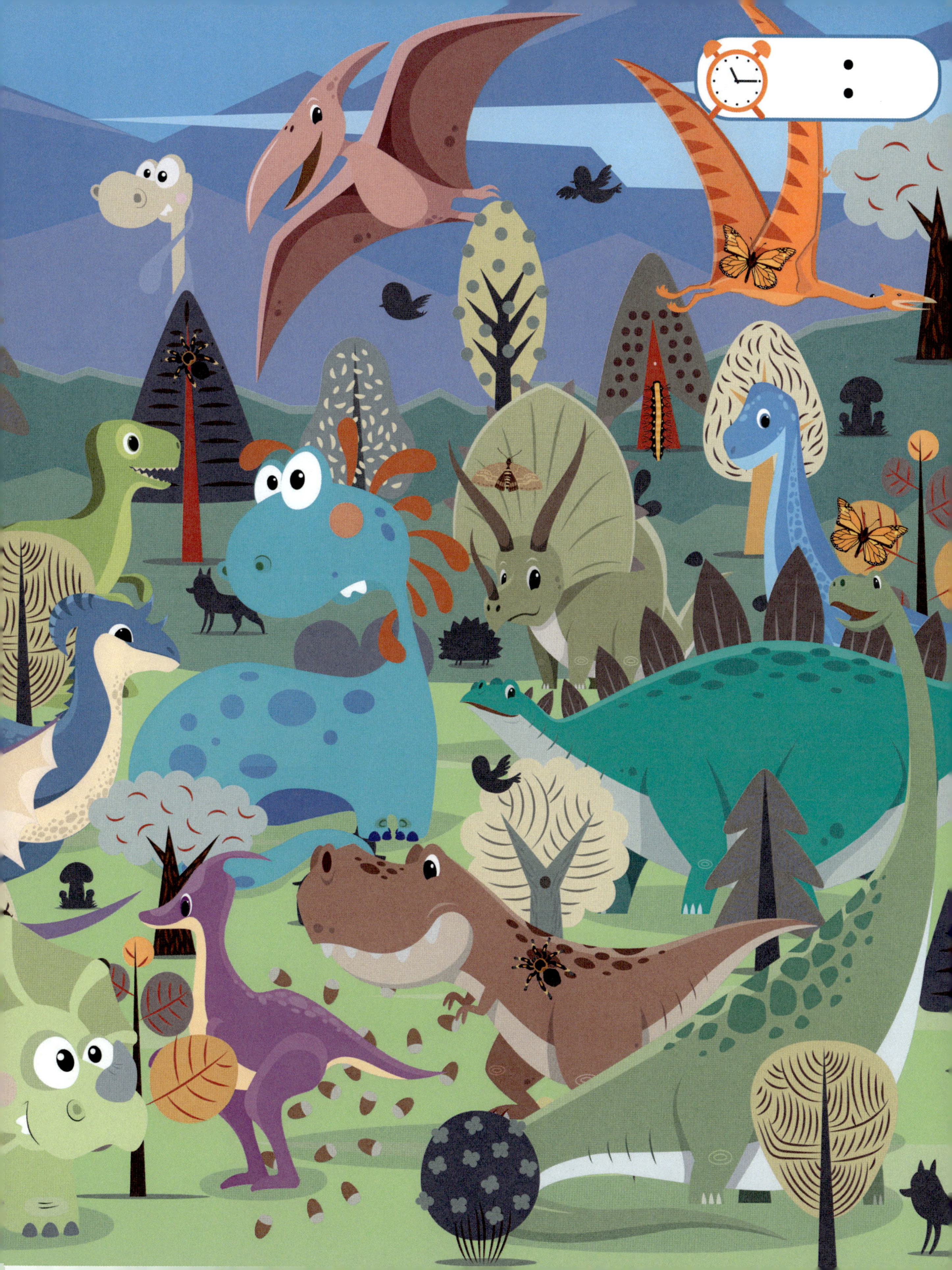

2 TRICERATOPS

3 STEGOSAURUS

3

3

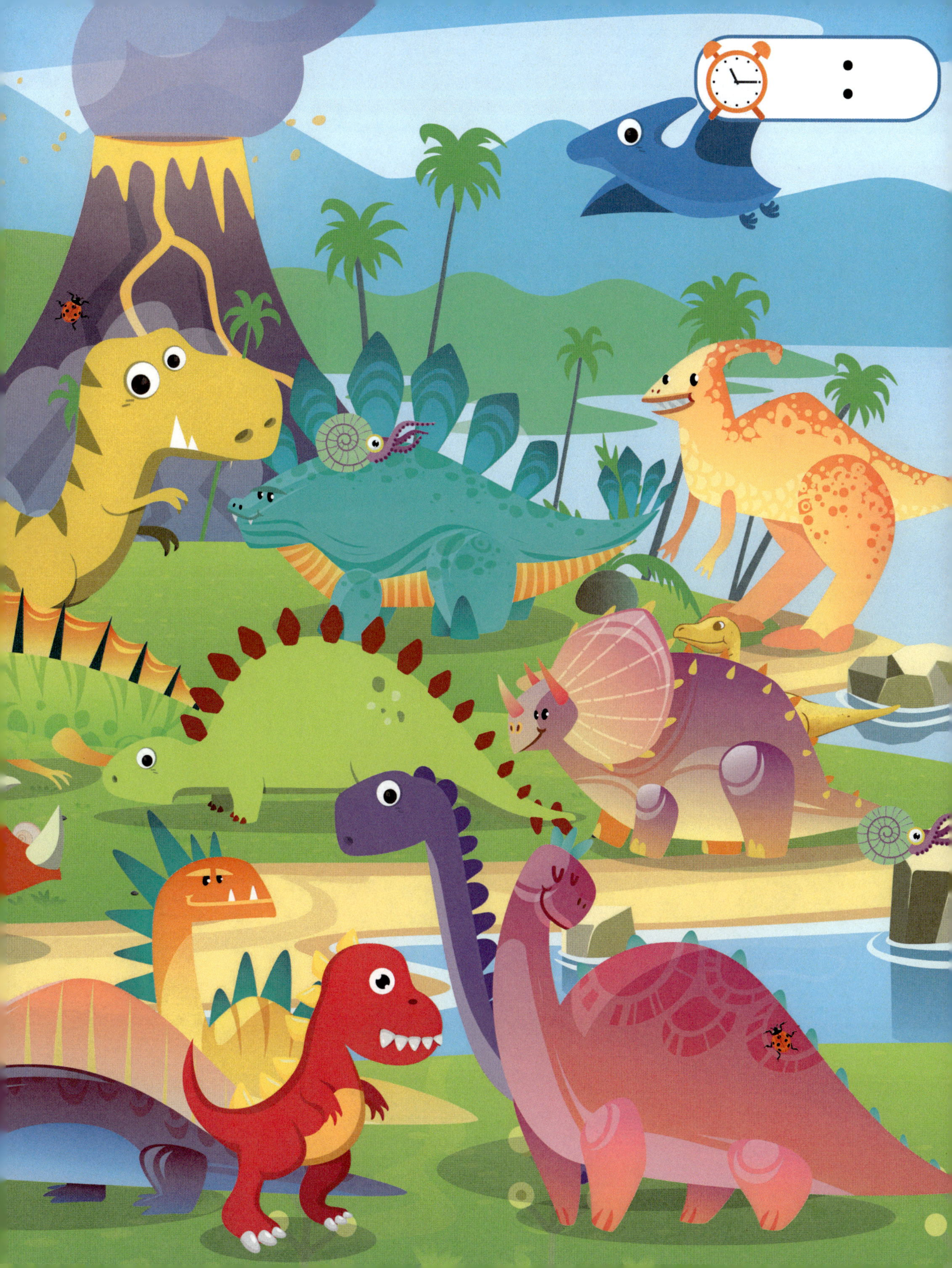

3
PARASAUROLOPHUS

1
T-REX

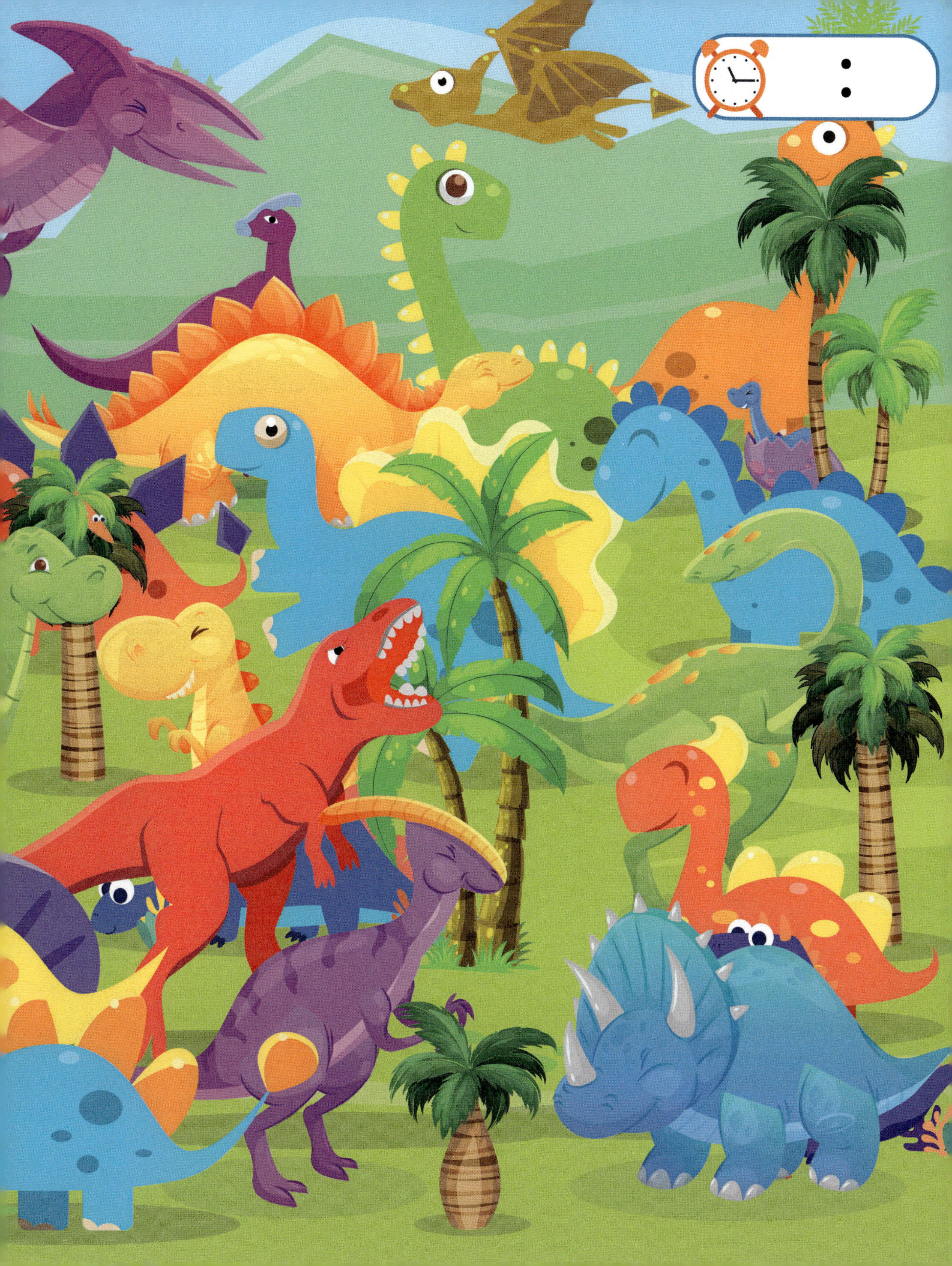

1 VELOCIRAPTOR

5 T-REX

3 DIPLODOCUS

1 ANKYLOSAURUS

Some dinosaurs could swim and fish.

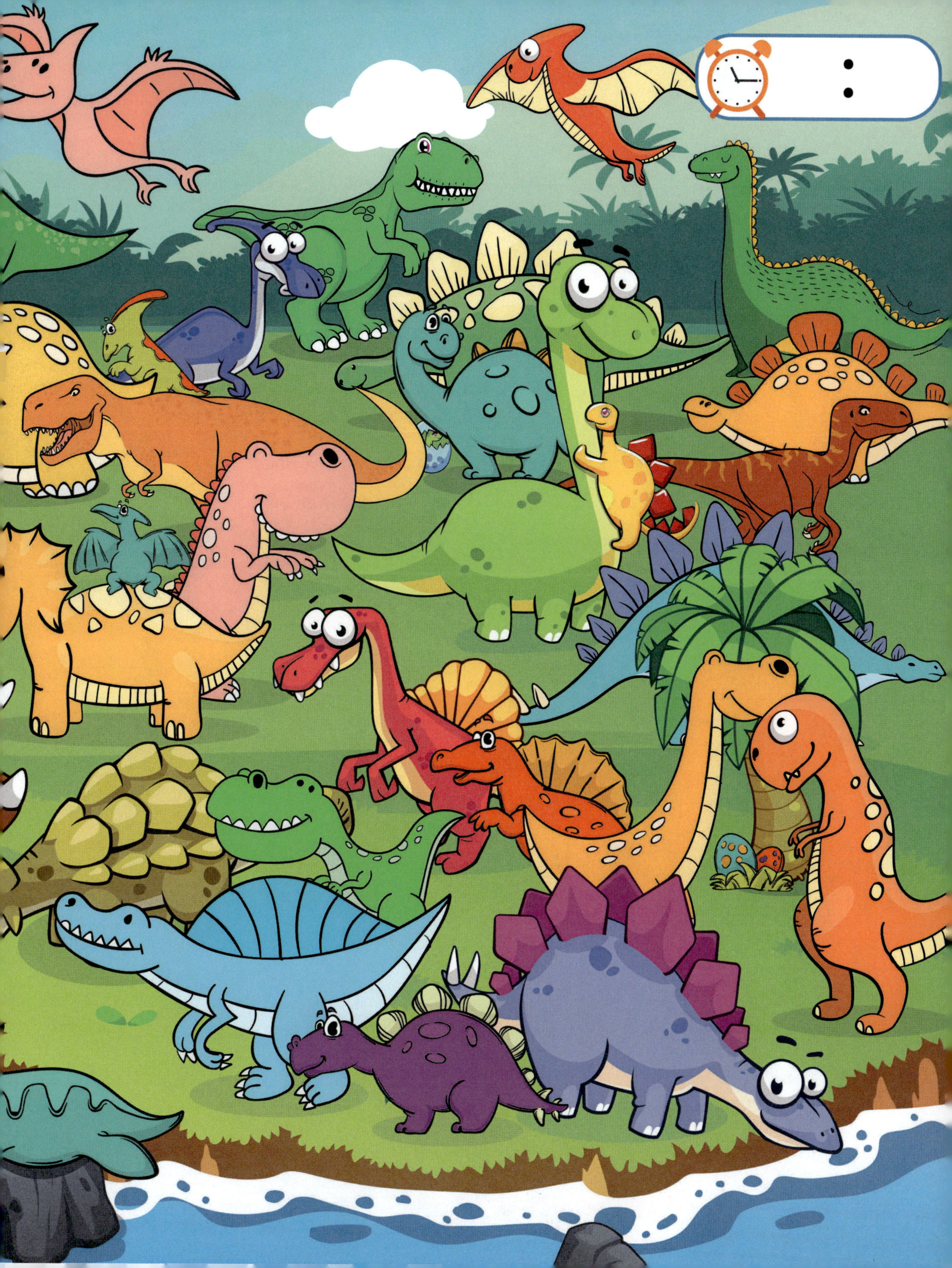

4

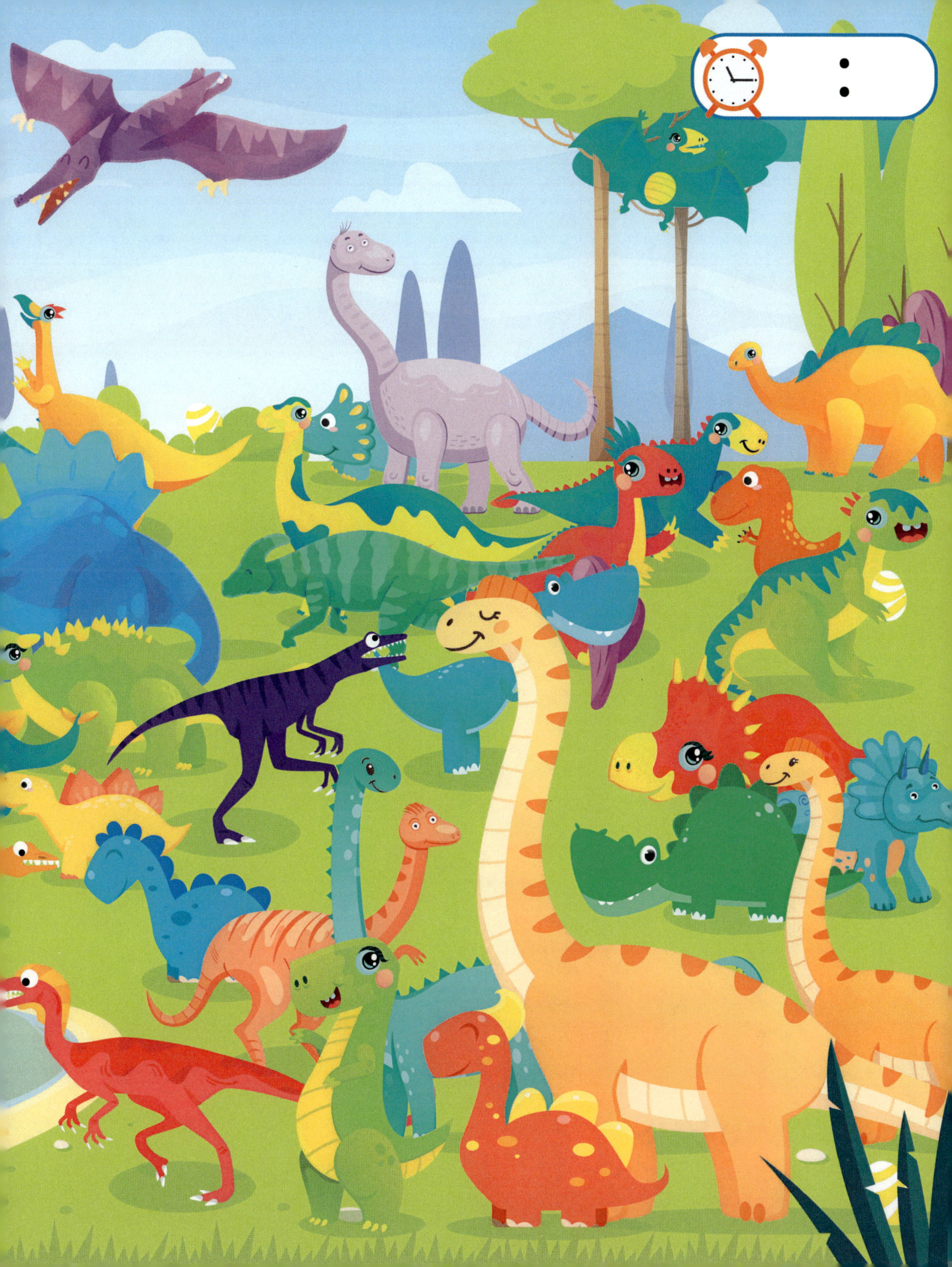

1
ANKYLOSAURUS

1
VELOCIRAPTOR

3
TRICERATOPS

BILLS

3 TRICERATOPS

2 DIPLODOCUS

The extinction of the dinosaurs was due to intense volcanic activity and a devastating meteorite impact.

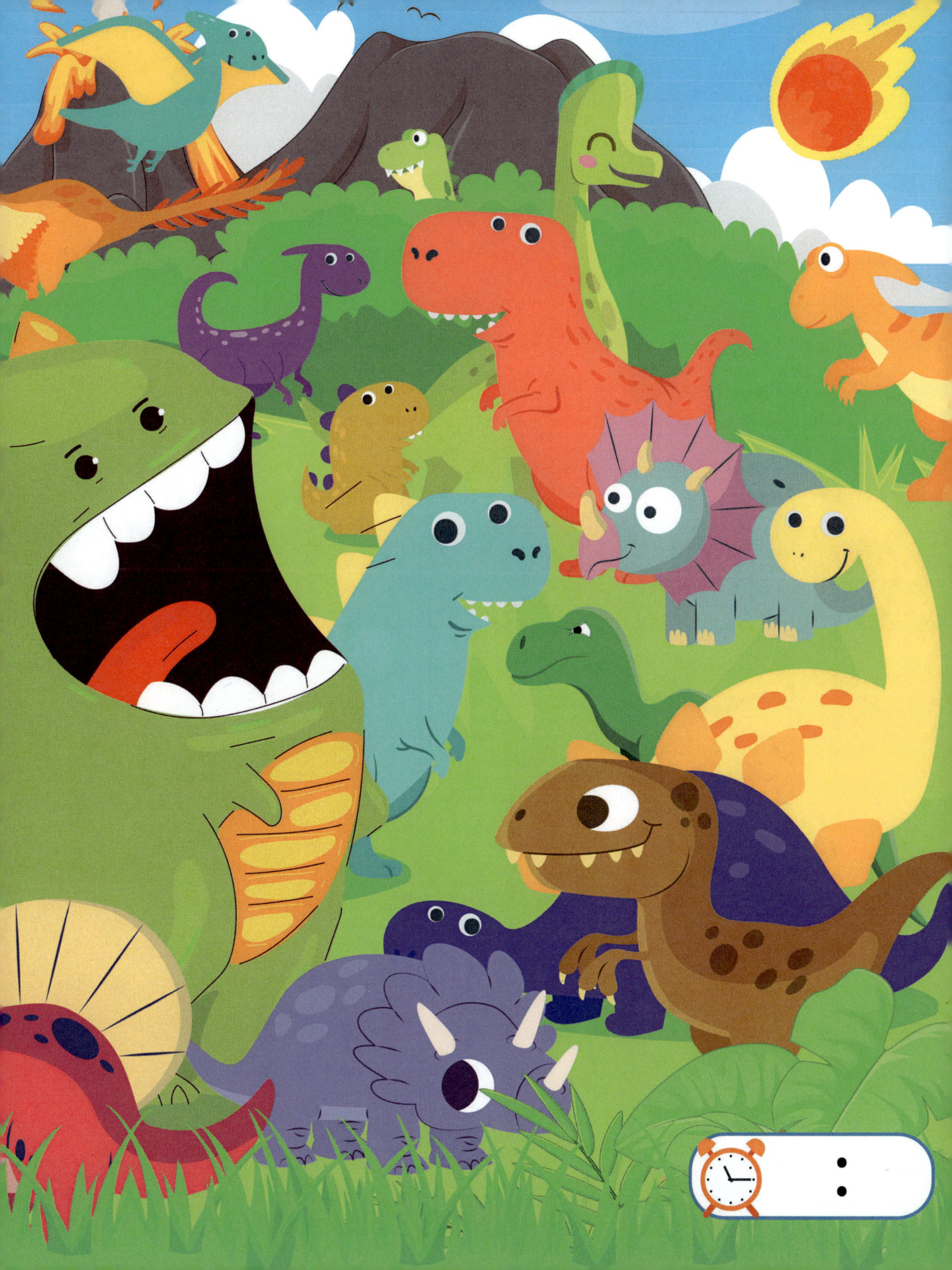

3

4

3

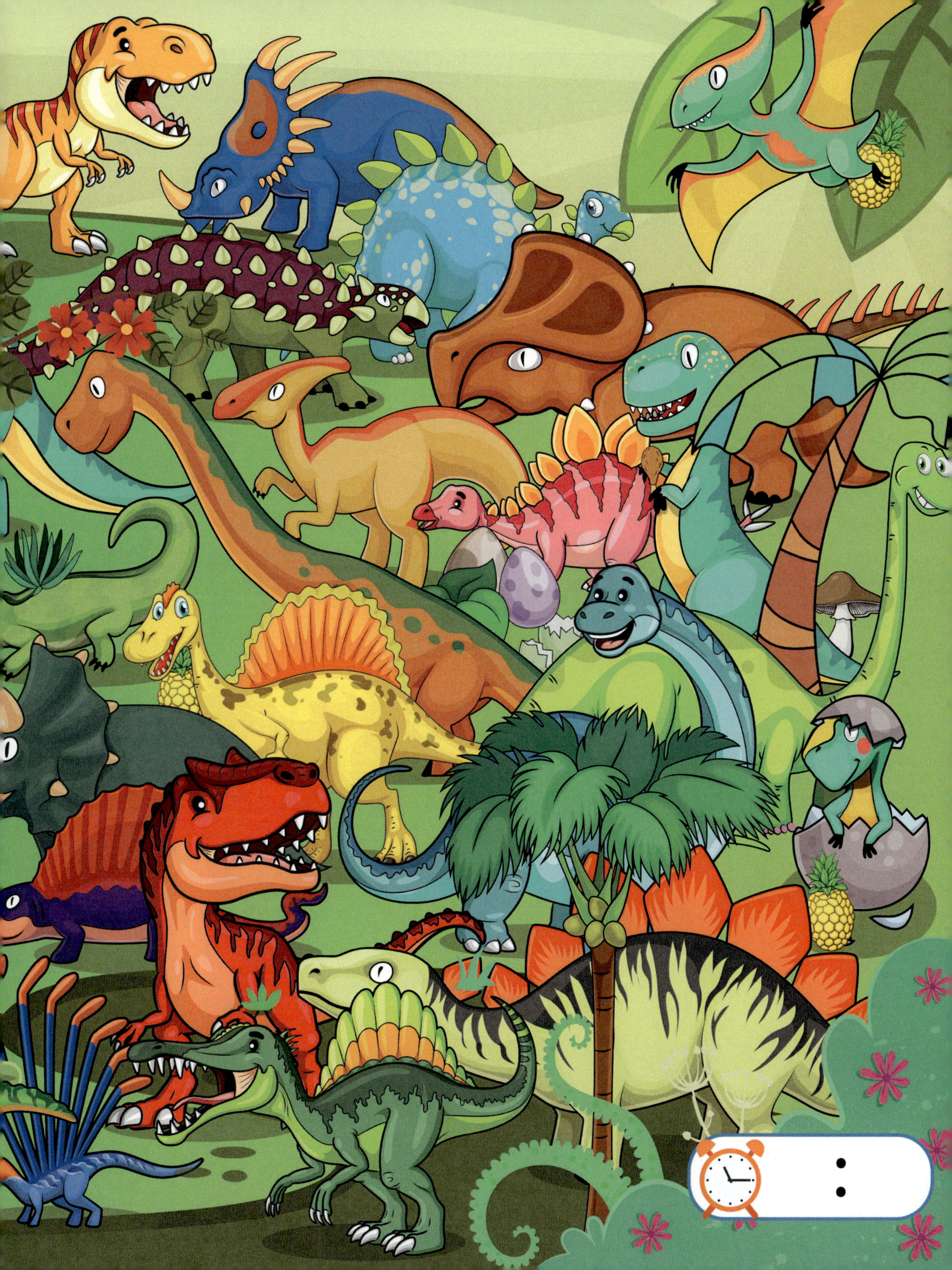

CHALLENGE SUCCEEDED!

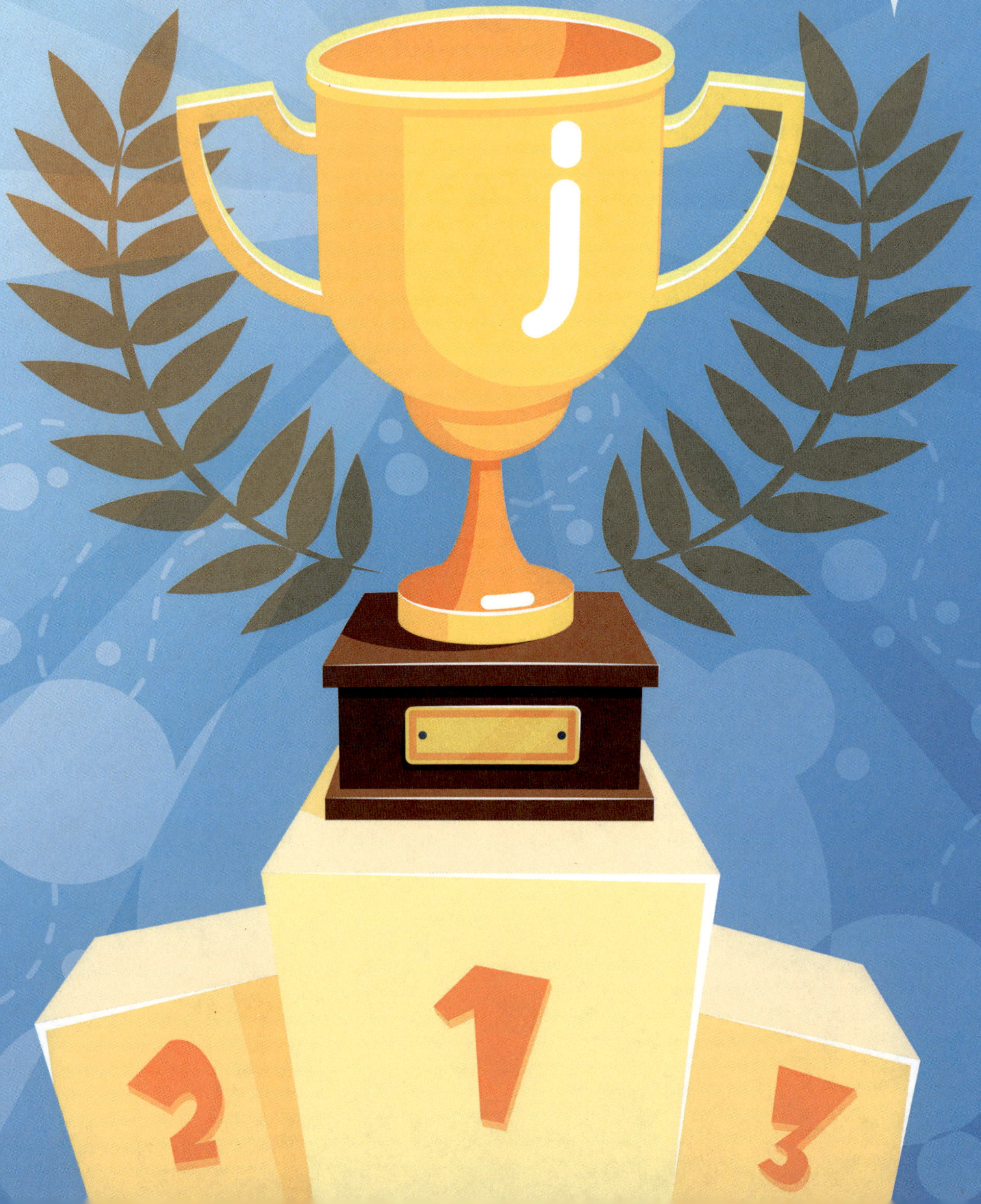

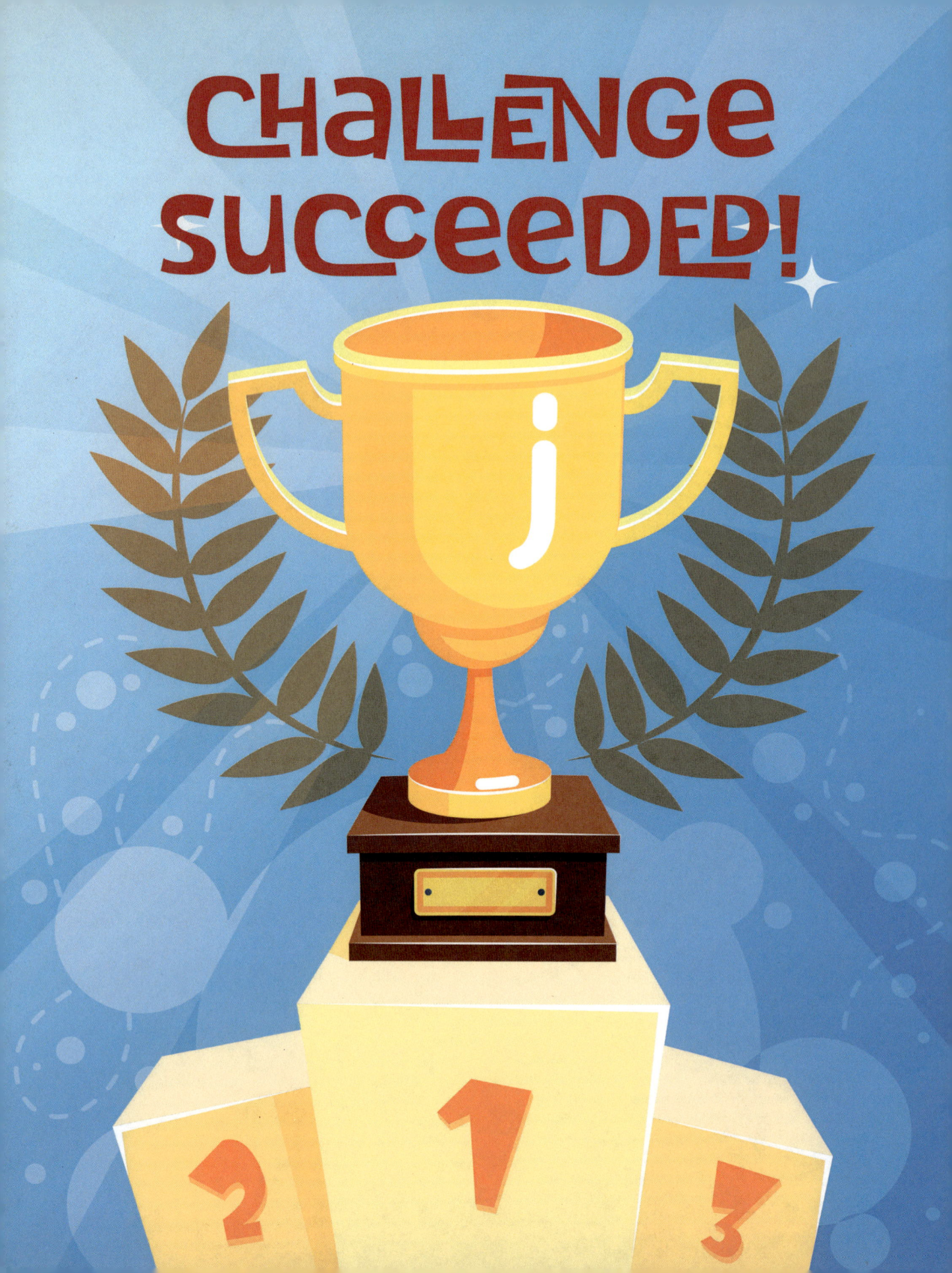

So if there are no more living dinosaurs, I have nothing to fear.

ACTIVITY GATO ©

YOU CAN RATE THIS BOOK OUT OF 5 STARS ON AMAZON. IT HELPS US A LOT !

CONTACT US ON: activitygato@gmail.com

YOU CAN FIND OUR OTHER BOOKS (MORE THAN 50 OTHER BOOKS) ON AMAZON BY TYPING «activity gato book»

see you next time !

Manufactured by Amazon.ca
Bolton, ON

28747426R00026